# Haiku Time
# Machine

Anne Consono

BookLeaf Publishing

India | USA | UK

Presentation by *BookLeaf Publishing*

Web: www.bookleafpub.com

E-mail: info@bookleafpub.com

ISBN: 9789360949211

First edition 2024

*Dedicated to the Sum of ALL the parts who have loved me.*

# ACKNOWLEDGEMENT

To all wandering souls trying to find their purpose who are not lost....

# PREFACE

Historical child hood growing up next to Lancaster county.

# Brandywine River

Dog days of summer

skipping rocks, with sleight of hand,

on the Brandywine.

# Cinder

As I watched her ride,

on a horse she named Cinder,

I longed to be her.

# Fowl Odor

Flapping, wings to perch

suddenly, the stench of flesh

electric fence wins.

# Thrashers at Ocean City

Salty memories

of greasy smiles, dripping

from boardwalk french fries.

# Mulberry

Stained lips, scraped knee,

up high in the Mulberry,

time seems to stop here.

# Worms

Flashlight passes,

over wet mounds of grass,

hunting for nightcrawlers.

# Haystack

Torrid grass of summer,

immense piles of haystacks ,

traverses my mind.

# Pearl

Poor pitiful Pearl

her sad eyes, piercing through me,

was my own reflection.

# Supper

Standing on a chair,

cast iron pops and sizzles,

supper is ready!

# Boothwyn

Boothwyn memories,

with Grandma, we slowly stroll,

through the market.

# Pigs in a blanket

Watching Grandma roll

cabbage, while she sang and danced,

for pigs in a blanket.

# Swimming

Launched into abyss,

a crystal blue persuasion,

I am baptized.

# Thunderstorm

My dreams don't want me,

writhing,twisted , nightmare storms

keeping me awake.

# Delaware River

Delaware River

A frozen aquarium,

December has come.

# Tobbogan

Stuffed like sardines,

our tin can, a tobbogan,

hurling, snow ocean.

# Sassafras

Smiling from my cheeks,

down the Sassafras river,

at last, I feel whole.

# Milk thistle

Snowstorm of flowers,

milk thistle bushes abuzz,

caught in it's silk web.

# Relievio

Invisible me!

humid ,summer nights we played,

nighttime hide n seek.

# Reading Railroad

Exhausting it's steam,

screeching to a sudden halt,

the tired train sighed.

# Chesapeake Bay

Sudden, stinging burn

clear, poisonous gelatin,

crawl to my blanket.

# Fireflies of Montchanin

Catching fireflies,

my sweating, innocent hands,

I am glowing.